My Mama's Garden

WRITTEN AND ILLUSTRATED BY MARY WILLIAMS

ISBN 9780999277348

www.creatingtolove.com

For John and Grace.
Thank you for teaching me
how to be a mama.
I love you!

Heartfelt gratitude to Kathy Ronan,
my mama, who taught me to love Mama Mary
and was an endless help with
and support of this book.

About the Children in this Book

 Jared

 Lily

 Violet

 Clem

 Fox

 Marigold

 Daisy

 William

Each of the children in this book is named after a flower traditionally found in Mary gardens. Like all children, they each have their own special interests and beautiful talents. Maybe you'll see yourself in one or more of them!

Jared means *Rose* in Hebrew. He loves playing with his dog and can't wait to be an astronaut when he grows up. He can tell you all kinds of facts about the solar system!

Violet has a most contagious giggle and carries her teddy bear everywhere she goes. She might be little, but she's strong of heart!

Daisy is an artist who loves drawing pictures of the flowers she picks in her yard. She's a little bit shy and a very loyal friend.

Fox is short for *Foxglove*. He loves books and often stays up past his bedtime to finish a chapter. He also loves writing and illustrating his own stories to read to his little brother and sister.

Lily loves wearing fancy dresses and running barefoot through the grass. She enjoys hosting tea parties with a side of mud pie! She's always the first one to offer a helping hand to someone in need.

Clem is a nickname for *Clemantis*. He dreams of being a professional baseball player. On a summer night, you would most likely find Clem having a campout in the treehouse he and his dad built.

Marigold is proud of her red hair, loves collecting stickers, and is always up for baking chocolate chip cookies. Her favorite activity is gymnastics. She can do 5 cartwheels in a row!

William is named for *Sweet William* of the dianthus flower family. He wants to be either a chef or a magician when he grows up. He's really good at telling knock knock jokes to make his friends laugh!

What is a Mary Garden?

A Mary garden is a beautiful way to honor Blessed Mother.

Several hundred years ago, scientists named plants

after Mary and her many wonderful virtues.

They used the herbs and flowers as a way to teach people about their faith.

Some common flowers found in Mary gardens

that you might find around your home, church, or neighborhood

include marigolds, roses, irises, lilies, carnations, and daisies.

The next time you add rosemary, chives, sage, or thyme to your food,

know that each of these is connected to

Mary in a very special way.

Anyone can set up a Mary garden to honor Our Lady!

Whether you plant flowers in your yard, grow some indoors in a pot,

or simply draw a colorful bouquet, Mama Mary knows of your love.

She will always wrap you in her mantle of God's grace.

My Mama's Garden

Whenever a worry makes my tummy feel funny,

when I'm not feeling well and my nose is all runny,

when joy fills my heart and prompts me to leap,

when I'm so excited and just can't sleep,

I go to my Mama's garden.

GARDEN

On a day when I'm feeling especially blue,

or when someone says things that are mean and untrue,

on a day when I'm grateful for the beauty I see,

or when I'm in awe of God's love for me,

I go to my Mama's garden.

With all
of the feelings
inside that I hide,

my Mama invites me to sit by her side.
She tenderly listens, my Heavenly Mother,
and lovingly brings me to Jesus, my Brother.

So....

let's go to my Mama's garden.

When I come to her garden, so lovely to see,

I first ask Our Lady what she wishes for me.

I show her my weeds of frustration and sadness,

she gives me new seeds of God's lasting gladness.

I turn over the soil, giving flowers more room,

to lift petals toward heaven and beautifully bloom.

Through every season, year after year,

whatever the weather, Mama stays near.

Sunrise to sunset she is by me each day,

her gentleness guides me in every way.

From her heavenly throne she sends showers of love,
her mantle protecting the world from above.

Wherever you are, remember and know,

Mama Mary is with you as you flourish and grow.

Maybe your garden is especially small,
just a hand-colored picture taped to a wall.

Maybe your garden is a windowsill pot,

where you often sit and think a lot.

If you don't have a garden to call your own,

no need to worry; you are still loved and known.

It's the garden you tend, that of your heart,

that thrives and blooms and sets you apart.

Your actions and words, your garden bouquet,

these are the flowers Mama puts on display.

Hail Mary, full of grace, my heavenly light,
be with me as I grow, help me do what is right.

You are with me each day awake or asleep;
you are always there, my journey to keep.

My love for you and your Son in my soul I will carry,
so I come to your garden, dear Mama Mary.

Hail Mary

Hail, Mary, full of grace,

the Lord is with thee.

Blessed art thou among women

and blessed is the fruit of thy womb, Jesus.

Holy Mary, Mother of God,

pray for us sinners,

now and at the hour of our death.

Amen.

Make a Mini Mary Garden

Color and cut out along the dotted lines.
Curl the long strips behind Mary
until they touch each other
and tape together.
Enjoy your mini Mary garden!

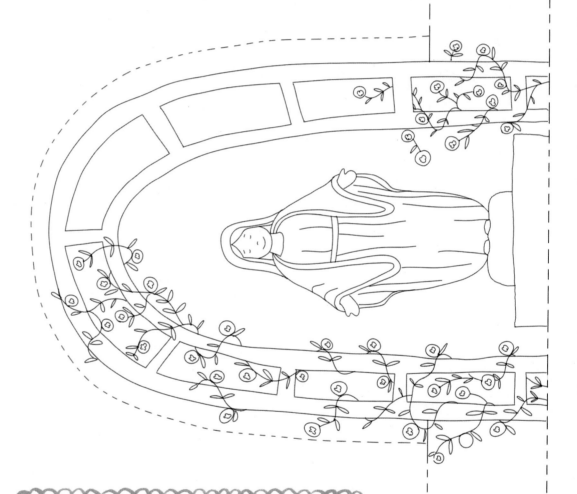

To download and print out
this activity page and more,
please visit
creatingtolove.com/mymamasgarden

About the Author and Illustrator

Mary Williams is a wife and
a mama of two beautiful children
and currently lives in Southern California.
She loves God, art, flowers,
and summertime adventures with her family.

You can find more of her work
at www.creatingtolove.com

My soul proclaims the greatness of the Lord;
my spirit rejoices in God my savior.
Luke 1:46-47

creating to love

www.creatingtolove.com
Instagram @creatingtolove
#creatingtolove

Made in the USA
Las Vegas, NV
30 March 2023